ENGLISH POTTED MEATS AND FISH PASTES

ELIZABETH DAVID

Published in 2023 by
Grub Street
4 Rainham Close
London
SW11 6SS

Email: food@grubstreet.co.uk
Twitter: @grub_street
Facebook: Grub Street Publishing
Instagram: grubstreetpublishinguk
Web: www.grubstreet.co.uk

Text copyright © Elizabeth David 1968, 1969
Copyright this edition © Grub Street 2023
Design: Myriam Bell

ISBN 978-1-911667-08-7

Printed and bound by Print Best, Estonia

Publishers note: The four booklets which constitute this set were first published by Elizabeth David Ltd for sale in her shop Kitchen Utensils, 46 Bourne Street, London SW1 in 1968 and 1969. They are reissued using the original texts which have not been updated.

CONTENTS

ENGLISH POTTED MEATS AND FISH PASTES

In the late 'forties and the early 'fifties, every new member of the Wine and Food Society received, together with a copy of the current number of the Society's quarterly magazine and a membership card, a pamphlet entitled *Pottery*, or *Home Made Potted Foods, Meat and Fish Pastes, Savoury Butters and Others*. The little booklet was a Wine and Food Society publication, the author's name was concealed under the whimsical pseudonym of 'A Potter', and the date was 1946.

The Wine and Food Society's propaganda in favour of homemade potted meats and fish was premature. In those days of rationing and imitation food we associated fish paste and potted meat with the fearful compounds of soya bean flour, dried egg and dehydrated onions bashed up with snoek or Spam which were cheerfully known as 'mock crab paste' and 'meat spread'. By 1954, when fourteen years of rationing came to an end none of us wanted to hear another word of the makeshift cooking which potted meats and fish pastes seemed to imply.

It was not until ten years later that we began to see that in fact these very English store-cupboard provisions, so far from being suited to the cheese-paring methods necessiated by desperate shortages, demand first class basic ingredients and a liberal hand with butter. It is indeed essential to understand that the whole success of the recipes described in this booklet depends upon these factors, and upon the correct balance of the ingredients.

Hungry as we are today for the luxury of authenticity and for visual elegance, we find that the Potter's work makes enticing reading:

"*How delicious to a schoolboy's healthy appetite sixty years ago, was a potted meat at breakfast in my grandmother's old Wiltshire home. Neat little white pots, with a crust of yellow butter suggesting the spicy treat beneath, beef, ham or tongue, handiwork of the second or third kitchenmaid ...*"

The Potter whose grandmother employed the second and third kitchenmaids in question was, M. André Simon tells me, Major Matthew Connolly (father of Mr. Cyril Connolly); and with his felicitous evocation of a mid-Victorian country breakfast table and those second and third kitchenmaids pounding away at the ham and tongue for potting he makes a number of points, most relevant of which concerns the kitchenmaids. What but the return of these handmaidens to our kitchens in the re-incarnated form of electric mixers, blenders and beaters[1] has made the revival of one of our most

---

1 Of these machines by far the most effective for potted meats, as also for raw pâté ingredients, is the recently introduced French Moulinette Automatic Chopper. This device does the job of chopping and pounding without emulsifying the ingredients or squeezing out their juices.

characteristic national delicacies a feasible proposition? Then, the neat little white pots, the crust of yellow butter, there is something fundamentally and uniquely English in the picture evoked by Major Connolly. It is a picture which belongs as much to the world of Beatrix Potter (Major Connolly would no doubt have appreciated the coincidental pun) as to that of the military gentleman from Bath, making it doubly an insult that the mass-produced pastes and sandwich spreads of the factories should go by the honourable names of potted meat, potted ham, tongue, lobster, salmon, shrimp and the rest.

Potted shrimps alone remain as the sole representative of these products to retain something of its original nature, although a few smoked haddock pastes are beginning to appear on London restaurant menus. These are usually somewhat absurdly listed as haddock pâté, or pâté de haddock fumé. In an expensive Chelsea restaurant I have even seen – and eaten – a mixture called *rillettes ecossaises* or 'pâté of Arbroath smokies with whisky'. The dish was good, but to label such a mixture rillettes when this is a word applicable exclusively to potted fat pork, or pork with goose or rabbit, does seem to touch the fringe of restaurateur's lunacy. For that matter, I find it sad that Arbroath smokies, the most delicate, expensive and rare of all the smoked haddock tribe, should be subjected to such treatment. Simply heated through in the oven with fresh butter, smokies are to me one of the most exquisite of our national specialities.

That crust of yellow butter so important to the true English potted meats and pastes as opposed to the Franglais and the factory-produced versions, does perhaps need a little more explanation than the late Major Connolly, who refers to it throughout his little work as 'melted butter', thought necessary to clarify. Clarified in fact is what it is, or should be, that butter. And since for the successful confection and storage of many, although not all, potted meats and fish, clarified butter is a necessary adjunct, it seems only fair to warn readers that the process does involve a little bother, although a trifling one compared to the services rendered by a supply of this highly satisfactory sealing, mixing, and incidentally, frying ingredient.

WHEN AND HOW TO SERVE POTTED FOODS AND PASTES

"A noble breakfast" says George Borrow of the morning meal offered him at an inn at Bala in North Wales, "there was tea and coffee, a goodly white loaf and butter, there were a couple of eggs and two mutton chops – there was boiled and pickled salmon – fried trout ... also potted trout and potted shrimps ..." A few weeks later he returns in search of more country delicacies. He is not disappointed. "What a breakfast! Pot of hare; ditto of trout; pot of prepared shrimps; dish of plain shrimps; tin of sardines; beautiful beef-steak; eggs, muffins, large loaf, and butter, not forgetting capital tea ..."

George Borrow was writing of *Wild Wales* in the eighteen-fifties. When you come to analyse his splendid breakfasts you find that with slight changes he might almost be describing a nineteen-sixties, chop-house revival period, West End restaurant lunch. The potted shrimps, the trout, the steak, the pot of hare (now the chef's *terrine de lièvre*) the mutton chops (now lamb cutlets) the salmon, now smoked rather than pickled, are very much with us still. The March of Progress has alas transformed the goodly white bread into that unique substance, restaurateur's toast, while tea and coffee are replaced by gin-and-tonic or a bottle of white wine, and for my part I would say none the worse for that. Tea with a fish breakfast or coffee with beefsteaks have never been my own great favourites in the game of what to drink with what.

Here we are then with plenty of ideas for an easy and simple English lunch; potted tongue or game followed by a simple hot egg dish; or smoked salmon paste with butter and brown bread to precede grilled lamb chops, or oven-baked sole, or fillet steak if you are rich. For a high tea or supper meal spread smoked haddock paste on fingers of hot toast and arrange them in a circle around a dish of scrambled eggs. For cocktail parties, use smoked salmon butter, fresh salmon paste, sardine or tunny fish butter, potted cheese, as fillings for the smallest of small sandwiches. Fish, meat and cheese pastes do not combine successfully with vol-au-vent cases, pastry or biscuits, but in sandwiches or spread on fingers of coarse brown bread they will be greeted as a blessed change from sticky canapés and messy dips. Stir a spoonful or two of potted crab or lobster (minus the butter covering) into fresh cream for *eggs en cocotte*, into a béchamel sauce to go over poached eggs or a gratin of sole fillets. And as Mrs. Johnstone, alias Meg Dods, author of the admirable *Housewife's Manual* of 1826 wrote, "What is left of the clarified butter (from potted lobster or crab) will be very relishing for sauces" while "any butter from potted tongue or chicken remaining uneaten will afterwards be useful for frying meat and for pastry for pies".

RECIPES FOR
POTTED MEATS

CLARIFIED BUTTER

In a large frying or sauté pan put a slab of butter (I use a good quality butter and find that it pays to prepare 2 lb at a time since it keeps almost indefinitely and is immeasurably superior to fresh butter for frying bread, croquettes, rissoles, fish cakes, veal escalopes, fish *à la meunière* and a score of other tricky cooking jobs). Let the butter melt over very gentle heat. It must not brown, but should be left to bubble for a few seconds before being removed from the heat and left to settle.

Have ready a piece of butter muslin wrung out in warm water, doubled, and laid in a sieve standing over the bowl or deep wide jar in which the butter is to be stored. Filter the butter while it is still warm. For storage keep the jar, covered, in the refrigerator.

The object of clarifying butter is to rid it of water, buttermilk sediment, salt and any foreign matter which for purposes of (a) frying cause the butter to blacken and burn, and (b) render it susceptible to eventual rancidity. The clarification process also expels air and causes the butter to solidify as it cools, making it a highly effective sealing material. In

French cookery clarified beef suet, pigs lard and goose fat are used in precisely the same way to seal pâtés and home-preserved pork and goose. These are the famous *confits* which are the French equivalents of our 18th and 19th century potted meat, game and poultry.

The delicious pork and goose *rillettes* and *rillons* of Western France are also close relations of English potted meats – in other words cooked and shredded or pounded meat packed into pots after cooking, as opposed to the pâtés and terrines which are made from raw ingredients cooked directly in the pots or the crust in which they are to be stored and served.

POTTED TONGUE

To my mind this is the best and most subtle of all English potted meat inventions. My recipe is adapted from John Farley's *The London Art of Cookery* published in 1783. Farley was master of the London Tavern, and an unusually lucid writer. One deduces that the cold table at the London Tavern must have been exceptionally good, for all Farley's sideboard dishes, cold pies, hams, spiced beef joints and potted meats are thought out with much care, are set down in detail and show a delicate and educated taste.

Ingredients and proportions for potted tongue are ½ lb each of cooked, brined and/or smoked ox tongue and clarified butter, a salt-spoonful of ground mace, a turn or two of black or white pepper from the mill.

Chop the tongue and, with 5 oz (weighed after clarifying) of the butter, reduce it to a paste in the blender or liquidiser, season it, pack it tightly down into a pot or pots, smooth over the top, cover, and leave in the refrigerator until very firm. Melt the remaining 3 oz of clarified butter and pour it, tepid, over the tongue paste, so that it sets in a sealing layer about one eighth of an inch thick. When completely cold, cover the pots. For short-term storage it is not necessary to keep potted tongue in the refrigerator, but it *is* desirable to serve it chilled.

If, therefore, the pots are stored in a larder, transfer them, as required, to the refrigerator for at least one hour before the meal.

Venison can be potted in the same way as tongue, and makes one of the best of all sandwich fillings. Salt beef makes another excellent potted meat.

TO POT HAM WITH CHICKENS

Readers interested in more than the bare formula of a dish will appreciate the charming, simple and well explained recipe below. Apart from the 18th century country house atmosphere evoked by the writing, we get also a very clear picture of the manner in which these potted meats were presented and a substantial hint as to the devising of other permutations and combinations of poultry, game and meat for potting:

"Take as much lean of boiled ham as you please, and half the quantity of fat, cut it as thin as possible, beat it very fine in a mortar, with a little oiled butter, beaten mace, pepper and salt, pot part of it into a china pot, then beat the white part of a fowl with a very little seasoning; it is to qualify the ham, put a lay of chicken, then one of ham, then chicken at the top, press it hard down, and when it is cold, pour clarified butter over it; when you send it to the table cut out a thin slice in the form of half a diamond, and lay it round the edge of your pot."

Elizabeth Raffald. *The Experienced English Housekeeper 1769.*

POTTED GAME

Grouse "potted whole, stowed singly into pots with clarified butter poured over" as described by Professor Saintsbury[2] (the old boy didn't miss much) are infinitely enticing, exceedingly extravagant with butter and not very practical for these days, but you can make one young cooked grouse or partridge go a very long way by the simple method of chopping the flesh, freed from all skin and sinew with about one quarter of its weight in mild, rather fat, cooked ham. You then put the chopped grouse and ham in the electric blender with 4 tablespoons of clarified butter to every ½ lb of the mixture. Add salt if necessary, a few grains of cayenne, a few drops of lemon juice. Reduce the mixture to a paste or purée. Pack it in to small straight-sided china, glazed earthenware or glass pots.

Put these into the refrigerator until the meat is very cold and firm. Then seal the pots with a layer of just-melted clarified butter.

Potted game is most delicious and delicate with hot thin, crisp brown toast for tea or as a first course at lunch.

It goes without saying that old birds can, equally, be used for potting, but they are much less delicate, need very long slow and thorough cooking, a larger proportion of fat ham (or pickled pork but not smoked bacon), and must be carefully drained of their cooking

---

2 In one of the *Fur, Feather and Fin* series of volumes published in the 1890s by Longmans, Green.

juices before they are prepared for chopping and pounding, otherwise sediment seeps through, collects at the bottom of the little jars and causes mould.

RILLETTES OR POTTED PORK IN THE FRENCH MANNER

This very famous charcutiers' or pork butchers' speciality is native to Southern Brittany, Anjou and Touraine. It could be described as the French equivalent of our potted meat – although it is very different in texture and taste.

2 lb of a cheap and fat cut of pork such as neck or belly; 1 lb of back pork fat; salt; 1 clove of garlic; two or three sprigs of dried wild thyme on the stalk; a couple of bay leaves; freshly milled black pepper.

Ask your butcher to remove the rind and the bones from the piece of pork meat (the bones can be added to stock and the rind will enrich a beef dish for the next course) and if he will, to cut the back pork fat into cubes.

Rub the meat with salt (about a couple of tablespoonsful) and let it stand overnight or at least a few hours before cutting it into 1½-inch thick strips – along the grooves left by the bones. Put these strips, and the fat, into an earthenware or other oven dish. In the centre put the crushed clove of garlic, the bay leaf and twig of thyme; mill a little black pepper over the meat and add about half a pint of cold water. Cover the pot. Place it in a very cool oven, gas 1, 290 deg.F. and leave for about 4 hours.

Now place a sieve over a big bowl. Turn meat and fat out into the sieve, so that all the liquid drips through. With two forks, pull apart the meat and fat (which should be soft as butter) so that the rillettes are shredded rather than in a paste. Pack the rillettes lightly into a glazed earthenware or stoneware jar of about ¾ pint capacity (or into two or three smaller jars). Taste for seasoning. Pour over the rillettes (taking care to leave the sediment) enough strained fat to fill the jar. Cool, cover and store in the refrigerator until needed.

Rillettes should be soft enough to spoon out, so remember to remove the jar several hours before dinner. Serve with bread or toast, with or without butter, as you please.

POTTED SPICED BEEF

With half a pound of cooked spiced beef including a good proportion of fat, and approximately 6 oz of clarified butter, a most excellent potted meat can be made. No extra spices are needed.

Cut the beef with its fat, into chunks, reduce them to paste in a blender or with an automatic chopper (see page 5), adding 3 oz of clarified butter as chopping proceeds.

Pack the paste into a pot or pots (it will fill a ¾ pint dish) press it well down, smooth the top with a palette knife, chill thoroughly before warming the remaining 3 oz of clarified butter, and pouring it over the top of the beef to form a complete seal.

Cover the pot or pots with foil and store in the refrigerator.

Potted meat should be eaten very cold with hot thin toast. Originally a breakfast dish, it makes a delicious first course for lunch.

RECIPES FOR POTTED FISH AND FISH PASTES

POTTED SALMON

Any woman who has salmon-fishing relations or friends will appreciate the point of this dish. Evolved at a time when salmon was comparatively cheap, and before the days of the tin and the refrigerated larder, potted salmon provided one method (pickling in wine and vinegar, salting, drying, kippering and smoking were others) of preserving surplus fish. Even today there will be readers who will be glad to know of a formula for dealing with a salmon or a piece of one received as a present, too big to be consumed immediately and likely to prove wearisome if eaten cold day after day.

For this recipe, evolved from instructions given in Elizabeth Raffald's *Experienced English Housekeeper* (an admirable book first published in 1769) all you need, apart from fresh salmon, are seasonings of salt, freshly milled white pepper, nutmeg, fresh butter and clarified butter.

Cut the salmon into thinnish steaks, arrange them in one layer in a well-buttered baking dish, sprinkle them with salt and seasonings, add about 1 oz of fresh butter, cut in pieces, for every pound of salmon, cover the dish with buttered paper and a lid, and put to cook in the centre of a moderately heated oven, gas No. 3, 330 deg.F. In 45 to 50 minutes – a little more or less according to the thickness of the steaks – the salmon will be cooked. Lift the steaks, very carefully, on to a wide sieve, colander or wire grid placed over a dish so that the cooking butter drains away.

Pack the salmon steaks into a wide dish or pot with the skin side showing. The dish or pot should be filled to capacity without being so crammed that the fish comes higher than the rim of the pot. I make my potted salmon in a shallow round white pot decorated on the outside with coloured fish. It is one of the old dishes especially made for potted char, the freshwater fish once a celebrated delicacy of the Cumberland Lake District. Cover with a piece of oiled foil or greaseproof paper and a board, or the base of one of the removable-base tart or cake tins now to be found in many kitchen utensil shops, to fit exactly inside the dish. Weight the board. Next day pour in clarified butter to cover the salmon and seal it completely.

Serve potted salmon in its own dish with a cucumber or green salad and perhaps jacket potatoes. A good luncheon or supper dish – and very decorative looking when cut at the table, into the cross-slices of which Elizabeth Raffald notes that "the skin makes them look ribbed".

SALMON PASTE

A more ordinary version of potted salmon can be made using cooked salmon and clarified butter in similar proportions and the same manner as for potted tongue (page 14). A salmon steak weighing about 7 oz will make a pot of salmon paste ample for four people, so it is a quite economical proposition.

POTTED CRAB

Extract all the meat from a freshly boiled crab weighing about 2 lb. Keep the creamy brown body meat separate from the flaked white claw meat. Season both with salt, freshly milled pepper, mace or nutmeg, cayenne, lemon juice.

Pack claw and body meat in alternate layers in small fire-proof pots. Press down closely. Pour in melted butter just to cover the meat.

Stand the pots in a baking tin of water, cook uncovered on the bottom shelf of a very low oven, gas No. 2, 310 deg.F. for 25 to 30 minutes.

When cold, seal with clarified butter. Serve well chilled.

Potted crab is very rich in flavour as well as in content, and is best appreciated quite on its own, perhaps as a midday dish served only with crisp dry toast, to be followed by a simple lettuce salad or freshly cooked green beans or purple-sprouting broccoli eaten when barely cold, with an oil and lemon dressing.

Those who find crab indigestible may be interested in the advice proffered by Merle's *Domestic Dictionary and Household Manual* of 1842, to the effect that after eating fresh crab it is always advisable to take "a very small quantity of good French brandy, mixed with its own bulk of water".

POTTED LOBSTER

Make in the same way as potted crab. Meg Dods (*The Cook's and Housewife's Manual* 1826) instructs that if this is to be kept as a cold relish the white meat and the coral and spawn should be packed "in a regular manner, in layers, or alternate pieces, so that when sliced it may have that marbled appearance, that look of mosaic work which so commends the taste of the cook".

SMOKED HADDOCK PASTE

Smoked haddock on the bone or in fillets, fresh butter, cayenne pepper, lemon.

Pour boiling water over the fish, cover it, leave ten minutes. Pour off the water, skin and flake the fish (taste it at this stage. If it is very salty, pour a second lot of boiling water over it). Weigh it. Mash it or purée it in the blender with an equal quantity of fresh unsalted butter. Season with plenty of lemon juice and a very little cayenne. No salt. Press into pots, cover, and store in the refrigerator.

I do not advise frozen haddock fillets for this paste. The false flavours of dye and chemical smoke are all too perceptible in the finished product.

There are restaurateurs and cookery journalists who like to call confections such as haddock and kipper paste by the name of pâté. I find this comical and also misleading.

KIPPER PASTE

As for smoked haddock. Smoked trout, mackerel and smoked cod's roe paste (not to be confused with the Greek taramasalata in which the cod's roe is mixed with olive oil and garlic) are also made in the same way, except that the boiling water treatment is superfluous.

SARDINE BUTTER

For this wonderfully simple little delicacy the sole requirements are good quality sardines in oil, fresh butter, lemon, and cayenne pepper. No clarified butter seal is necessary.

Drain off the oil. Skin and bone the sardines. To each large sardine allow a scant ounce of butter, ½ oz if the sardines are small. Mix butter and sardines very thoroughly, mashing them with a fork until you have a smooth paste. Season with a few drops of lemon juice and a sprinkling of cayenne pepper.

Pack the sardine butter into small pots, cover, store in the refrigerator, serve well chilled, with thin, crisp brown toast.

SMOKED SALMON BUTTER

Make this in the same way as sardine butter, using the same proportions of fish and butter. It is an excellent way of turning a second grade smoked salmon, i.e. imported Canadian or Norwegian, or a few slices cut from the end of a side (sometimes sold cheaply by fishmongers and delicatessen merchants) into a real delicacy. If possible, use unsalted or only very slightly salted butter. A good deal of lemon juice will be needed.

For a first course for four, 6 oz each of salmon and butter is a plentiful allowance.

Have lemons and a pepper mill on the table and toast as for sardine butter.

TUNNY FISH BUTTER

Same again. But pick your brand of tunny carefully. It isn't worth wasting butter or work on coarse dark tunny. About the best English-packed brand is Epicure. The Portuguese Nice is better.

COD'S ROE PASTE IN THE GREEK MANNER

Cheap, easy, made in advance, an admirable standby. What you can do with a two-ounce jar of smoked cod's roe, a few spoonfuls of oil and a potato is quite a revelation to many people.

For a 2 oz jar of smoked cod's roe the other ingredients are about 4 tablespoons of olive oil, a medium-sized potato, lemon juice, cayenne pepper, and water; and, optionally, a clove of garlic.

An hour or two before you are going to make the paste, or the evening before if it's more convenient, turn the contents of the jar into a bowl, break it up, and put about 3 tablespoons of cold water with it. This softens it and makes it much easier to work. Drain off the water before starting work on the making of the dish.

Pound the garlic and mash it with the cod's roe until the paste is quite smooth before gradually adding three tablespoons of the oil. Boil the potato without salt, mash it smooth with the rest of the oil, combine the two mixtures, stir again until quite free from lumps, add the juice of half a lemon and a scrap of cayenne pepper. Pack the mixture into little pots or jars. Serve chilled with hot dry toast. Enough for four.

This little dish, or a similar one, is now listed on the menus of scores of Cypriot-Greek taverns and London bistros under the name of taramasalata. It is indeed very much akin to the famous Greek speciality, except that true taramasalata is made from a cod's roe much more salty, more pungent, and less smoked than our own. There is also a great deal more garlic in the Greek version, and very often bread instead of potato is used as a softening agent.

INDEX OF RECIPES